THE CHRISTIAN FAITH THE SAFEGUARD OF FREEDOM.

A THANKSGIVING SERMON;

PREACHED IN THE

PRESBYTERIAN CHURCH

OF

ANTRIM, N. H.

NOVEMBER 29th, 1855.

BY

J. H. BATES.

NEW YORK:
HOWARD F. SNOWDEN, PRINTER, 162 PEARL STREET.
1856.

THE CHRISTIAN FAITH THE SAFEGUARD OF FREEDOM.

A THANKSGIVING SERMON;

PREACHED IN THE

PRESBYTERIAN CHURCH

OF

ANTRIM, N. H.

NOVEMBER 29th, 1855.

BY

J. H. BATES.

NEW YORK:
HOWARD F. SNOWDEN, PRINTER, 162 PEARL STREET.
1856.

PREFATORY NOTICE.

The following discourse, though originally designed by the author only for the people of his own charge, is now very respectfully dedicated to all the members of the congregations under the care of Lodonderry Presbytery. It is published in the hope that it may win a stronger and more intelligent affection for the pure doctrines of the gospel, and for the Presbyterian church; so far as that church is found to have been, and to be, the uncompromising defender of those doctrines. There has been no desire to institute any comparison, derogatory to the just claims of other churches, but simply to draw legitimate conclusions from the unalterable facts of the past. It is believed that these *facts*, in their bearing upon each other and upon the progressive amelioration of the world's sufferings, distinctly declare the truth and the will of God. If history point directly to the Presbyterian church, as God's more favored agency in defending and propagating that truth which can alone sanctify men's hearts and regenerate the world, such fact is sufficient of itself, to commend our church to favorable regard; and the earnest conviction that such is the fact, must exonorate the author of this discourse, in the minds of all candid persons, from the charge of mere sectarian zeal.

One further object is aimed at in this publication. It is hoped that intelligent men of the world, who manifest little or no interest in the church of Christ, will discover their unreasonable ingratitude, in withholding their support from that gospel which, by its transforming and energizing power, has secured for them the highest civil and social blessings they enjoy. It is hoped that they, for the sake of the world at large and coming generations, will come to feel their duty to aid in the extension of that ancient faith of the saints, which has ever shown itself at war with spiritual despotism, and has taught the true value of those institutions of civil freedom, which are the only safeguard against human aggression upon the highest and dearest rights which God has given to man. Infidelity and some forms of religious belief, while they have promised a larger liberty, have in fact only begotten a stronger bondage. They have shut off the sanctifying influences of divine truth from the hearts of men: they have broken down the barriers which truth has placed to corrupt passions: they have left depravity to work out its natural results: they have strengthened the tyranny of sin over the human soul: they have indeed given a larger liberty to the wicked and cruel passions of men, but left the world to a corresponding increase of suffering. The true faith of the saints has ever been at work to advance the highest good of man. What friend of his race, what lover of constitutional freedom, will withhold his support from the pure doctrines of the gospel?

SERMON.

Text: Jude 3. *Contend earnestly for the faith which was once delivered to the Saints.*

The contest, enjoined by the text, has been no less a contest for human freedom than for religious truth. The Apostle, in a general address to christians, says, "Contend." And for what? Not for the world's wealth or pleasure or glory. He had no need to exhort to a contest for either of these. "Contend for the faith." And what faith? Not for human opinions; not for the dogmas of any earth-born philosophy. Many, without any entreaty, have ever been found ready to enter this field of warfare. But "contend for the faith which was once delivered to the saints." Explain and defend those truths which God has, at sundry times, revealed to his servants and his people, for their well-being and the well-being of the world. And *how* contend? Earnestly,—not slothfully nor indifferently, but earnestly, with the whole soul.

And men have contended. They have sacrificed ease and pleasure and wealth and all that the world calls glory and honor, yea and life too in the conflict. They have contended with earnestness. They would have sooner given up everything else than the truth of God. Great multitudes have died in the struggle. Others have come after them to enjoy the blessed fruits of the victory: and we, here assembled to-day, are among the most favored heirs to that inestimable inheritance which has been purchased at the expense of rivers of christian blood.

What are our blessings to-day, for which we ought to be most thankful? We look at our garners and praise God for the bounty with which he has crowned the rolling year. We call to mind the Lord's preserving care over us. The fatal pestilence, which elsewhere has brought death and desolation, and sorrow and woe, into many a heart and many a home, has not been suffered to come near us. We praise God for his goodness. Elsewhere cruel war has devastated fair cities, filled them with carnage, strewn the earth with human corpses and enriched the ground with human gore; while we have reason to bless the Lord for the peace that has been upon almost all our borders. Other nations have been distracted with anarchy and dissension, but, though we have reason to take to ourselves shame for some local broils, in connection with the elective franchise, we thank God for the great quietness that has reigned within all our coasts. Some fearful and fatal calamities have met multitudes in the midst of life's career and sent a momentary sadness into the public heart; and yet we may justly call upon our souls to thank the Lord for our nation's happiness and prosperity.

We are indeed at no loss to find reasons for thanksgiving. The rich and numerous mercies of the closing year are enough to penetrate the soul with the deepest feelings of gratitude. But what is it that greatly enhances the value of the daily care of Providence in bestowing health and food and raiment and social privileges? Is not this kind guardianship of Heaven made a hundred fold more blessed, from the fact that we can enjoy it in peace? Is not our exemption from oppression, both civil and spiritual, a most important part of the daily goodness which we receive at the hands of a gracious God?

While then we make grateful mention of the kindnesses of the Lord, let us not forget our freedom; not the mere liberty to seek our temporal happiness in our own way: but the liberty to *think* and to act according to our convictions of right; the liberty to obey conscience, and God. For what freedom can you have if the soul be enslaved? What liberty is worth the name, if, under penalty of fines, imprisonment, torture and death, you are forbidden to worship God according to his revealed will, and seek his glory as the divinely prescribed end of your being? Talk not of freedom, says he whose soul has been freed from the bondage of sin, if I may not learn the truth of God and obey it; yea talk not of life, if I may not employ it for the honor of my God, and my soul's eternal good. What man was ever free whose soul was bound in fetters, forged and clenched by human power? What nation was ever free, where the rights of conscience were not safe against all human encroachment? What people ever possessed true civil liberty, when the privilege was denied them of receiving and obeying that form of doctrine which was once delivered to the saints?

But who built this glorious temple of freedom in which we worship to-day? The frame-work is God's; the covering, the ceiling, the furnishing are all his. But did it come to us entire? Was it let down from Paradise in all its completeness? Far otherwise. Its foundations were laid in darkness and gloom. The underworkmen were persecuted, tormented, slain. The Master Builder was buffeted, tortured and crucified; and human tyranny has left no expedient untried to effect its destruction. But still the work went on, and to-day we sing the hymn of grateful praise and bend the suppliant knee beneath its vaulted roof, whose height reaches to the heavens, and whose extent spans one of the broadest empires on the globe.

Is it not meet that we should stop to admire the goodliness of this building? What columns! How grand, how lofty, how exquisitely adorned by art divine! That dome, how stately! How towering high that pinnacle, reaching even to the throne of God! Surely it is good to be in such a place. Let us here worship God and praise him for his goodness. Let us lift up holy hands toward Heaven and call upon our souls to join the joyful shout, The Lord reigneth! The Lord reigneth! And none may molest us or make us afraid, while we yield to his mild and righteous sway. Here we may have some foretaste of that freedom which saints alone enjoy, who worship in spirit and in truth to perfection, within that gorgeous temple whose maker and builder is God.

Civil freedom, regulated by law and reason, and the rights of conscience are the gifts of heaven and the birthright of man. They are inalienable blessings and cannot be bartered away without violating the first condition of their bestowment. They were given for our possession and enjoyment and not for our disposal. We have been so accustomed to them that we scarcely realize the possibility of their being lost. We almost forget that any have ever suffered from their denial, and so greatly fail to appreciate the worth of our blessings. But how was it when Jesus died under Pontius Pilate? How was it when the Apostles were constrained to assert the right and the duty to obey God rather than man? How was it during those ages of gloom when Pagan powers hunted and destroyed the followers of Christ, as ravenous beasts are hunted and destroyed?

How was it during that dark night in the world's history, when Popery, wielding the double sceptre of church and state, had well nigh driven truth and piety from the earth? How was it during that "reign of terror," when atheistic France decreed there was no God, abolished the holy sabbath and with fiendish shouts destroyed the sanctuaries of the Lord? How was it in Holland, where more than fifty thousand Belgic Martyrs perished by the hands of the Spaniards?* How was it in England when multitudes of the most worthy of the clergy were driven into poverty and exile, for non-conformity in the trifling matter of surplice and litany, or burned at the stake for defending the truth of God? How in Scotland, when a remorseless hireling soldiery, like prowling beasts of prey, sought for the faithful Covenanters amid the fastnesses of their heath-covered hills? How was it when the false prophet, by means of fire and sword, forced upon unwilling nations the religion of the Koran? How is it at this day in Papal Tuscany or Lutheran Sweden, where no one may think differently from the religion established by law? Study these histories, if you would know the blessedness of religious freedom.

And why to day, are we not groaning under a like oppression? Who and what maketh us to differ? God, who gloriously ruleth over all for-ever-more, has placed a difference between this and past ages, between this and other lands. Why he has made such difference between the equally worthy creatures of his hands, and subjects of his kingdom, we may not decide, but we may appropriately examine the means by which he has done it, as it may help to determine the path of duty for us.

God works by means, no less in the moral than in the natural world, and he has proposed to Himself two great ends, viz: the restoration of the human soul from the misery of the fall, and the recovery of the world from the wretchedness which sin has entailed upon it. The misery of the fallen soul shows itself in the corruption of man's heart and the wickedness of his life. The wretchedness of the world is seen most conspicuously in the wrong and oppression which one part of mankind has practised upon the other part. The merciful purposes of God are accomplished when men are sanctified through the agency of divine truth, and society makes progress in

*See Dr. Spring's "Power of the Pulpit."

the order of christian civilization, whereby the proper rights of man are defined and secured.

With respect to the constitutional security for human rights, we cannot but discover a decided difference, favorable to ourselves, between this nation and most other nations of the past and the present. And we may ask, and ought to ask, what has produced this difference? We justly ascribe honor to the Fathers of our Revolution. We would brand as an unworthy son of freedom, the man who failed to revere the memory of those noble patriots who pledged and hazarded their fortunes and their lives in defence of American Independence. But who taught our fathers the true principles of liberty? Who instilled into their minds a hatred of injustice, though it were shown only in the trifling matter of a tax on tea or stamped paper? Who taught them that the principle of right once yielded, opens the floodgate of oppression? Who instructed them that the rights of conscience should be held sacred against all human aggression? Who told them that there would be extreme danger to the peace and happiness of the nation unless religious freedom were guaranteed to all by constitutional enactment? Who had the training of our Fathers of the Revolution?

This is a legitimate question. We justly honor the man, who, by his talents and moral virtues, lays the world under obligation;—but shall we forget the father, the mother or the teacher, by whom those talents were cultivated and those virtuous principles implanted? King Maximillian, of Bavaria, erects a costly monument to the memory of his teacher, the philosopher, Schelling, and we cannot but commend this tribute of affection. Let us not forget the instructors of our fathers, who inspired them with the love of truth and virtue, and nerved their hearts and hands for fierce conflict in their defence.

But who were they, that we may do them honor? I answer, such men as PETER and STEPHEN and PAUL and Justin and Polycarp and the host of sainted martyrs who perished, during the first three centuries of the christian era, at the instigation of Pagan Emperors and Magistrates. During the dark ages which succeeded the corruption of the church by its union with the civil power, there were many persecuted christians who bore witness to the truth. And then came Luther and Melancthon and Zuingle and Farrel and Calvin and Knox and Latimer and Ridley, and a host of reformers of the continent and of Britain. These men, living in the faith and dying in the faith, most of them for the faith, bore testimony against human oppression in the holy name of religion, and sealed their testimony with suffering and death. Faithful christian men, from the days of Christ until now, who have, in the face of violent opposition and in spite of the most cruel persecution which fiend-like hearts could invent, earnestly contended for the faith once delivered to the saints, have been teachers in the great principles of human freedom. And they have been more than teachers. At the expense of the greatest sacrifices that man can make, they have purchased and transmitted all the true liberty the world at this day enjoys. Where would have been human freedom if the Apostles, in obedience to the commands of the ruling powers, had ceased to speak in the name of Jesus? Where would have been freedom if the primitive christians had abandoned their faith because heathen tyrants demanded it? How intensely dark, without a cheering star, and without a presage of a coming dawn, would have been the world's moral night, had there been none who dared to maintain the faith of the saints against the spiritual tyranny of the man of sin! Had there been no Luther, with his lion-hearted boldness, to attack the errors and vices and worse than heathen follies of Rome; had there been no Melancthon, with his powerful mildness, sweetly to win men to the truth; had there been no Calvin, with his irresistible logic, to explain and defend the doctrines of grace; had there been no Knox, who could send terror to the heart of the British Queen, if he did but approach God in prayer;—had there been no such men, earnestly to contend for the christian faith, the nations of the earth might still have been enveloped in moral night and groaning under the oppressive heel of tyranny.

Do you doubt it? Study then the past, study its doings and its achievements in connection with its religious opinions. It is impossible to understand civil history if it be separated from religious history. To study history, disconnected from religion, is like studying the structure and phenomena of the human body, leaving out the heart and the lungs. There are fluids, flowing through all parts of the system, affording needed nourishment everywhere and carrying off whatever may be superfluous and injurious. But what sends forth the blood and calls it back and fits it for its office of purging and strengthening? Here must be a profound mystery, until we learn the functions of the heart and lungs. So in the political world. Changes are effected. The enslaving shackles of despotism are loosened. There is a gradual emerging from the folly and superstition of heathenism to the active intelligence of christian civilization. Revolutions take place; forms succeed forms and dynasty follows dynasty. But whence comes all this? We enquire in vain until we search the arcana of religion. As with the individual, so with the nation. Whatever religion a man receives he receives it into the heart, and his outward life is affected by it. *As a man thinketh in his heart, so is he.* In other words, a man is what his religious sentiments make him to be. So with the State. Whatever religion it has, occupies the heart of the people and controls those political phenomena which strike the world's senses.

The deepest feelings of man are his *religious* feelings, and it is these which give direction to his external acts. It is so with him whether he act alone or as a constituent part of community. Society has a heart and is moved by its feelings and dictates as well as the individual. Ambitious politicians have understood this truth and have turned it to the account of their ambitious schemes. Statesmen have known it and calculated upon it in their plans for national prosperity and aggrandisement. If we would decide upon the character of the state, we must know the condition of the heart and what religious sentiments prevail there. If we would study history aright, we must study it in connection with religious opinions. The worst sufferings, that men have ever endured, have been inflicted in the abused name of religion. The noblest specimens of heroic daring, the world has ever witnesed, have been exhibited in the holy cause of religion.

Would you have a specimen? Luther was cited to the Diet of Worms, to answer for his religious doctrines. His friends warned him of the plots of his enemies, but in spite of all entreaties he declared his purpose to attend the Diet, though he should meet as many devils as there were tiles upon the roofs of the city. Nor was this an empty boast; he understood his danger and knew whereof be affirmed. But who was it that put the Reformer's life in jeopardy? Men who were actuated by hearts filled with a false religion. And what was it that nerved the soul of Luther to meet such danger? It was the religion of Jesus, the faith once delivered to the saints.

Would you have other specimens? History abounds in them. We will select from events in the reign of Louis XIV. The soldiery seized a man, by name Isaac Favin, and, having suspended him by his arm pits, tormented him for a whole night, by tearing his flesh with pincers. The gratification of a cruel spirit was their only reward. A boy of the tender age of twelve years was surrounded with faggots. Amid the tortures of the flames he cried out, "My God, help me." He did not seek the assistance of a fiendish soldiery by renouncing his religion. Mothers were kept fast to posts, while for days and nights their helpless babes were famishing for food and gasping for life before their eyes. What was it that steeled the hearts of a soldiery and a priesthood against all feeling of humanity and enabled them to find matter for laughter and sport in scenes of cruelty at which barbarism itself should weep? *A false religion.* And what was it with which men, women and children girded the loins of their minds for the enduring of such fiery trials? These were all martyrs for the truth as it is in Jesus. They suffered in an earnest contest for the faith once delivered to the saints. The faith, for which they suffered, armed them for the conflict; it brought heavenly assistance and took away the fear of pain and death by opening to their vision the bright vistas of a future world.

These examples set in striking contrast the effects of a false religion and the true. They show how the one degrades and brutefies humanity, while the other purifies and enlarges the soul for a compliance with those holy precepts which distinguish the religion of the Bible from every other form of doctrine, and for a participation in those heavenly thoughts and feelings which distinguish the child of God from an heir of Hell.

These examples show how hardened and cruel the heart may become when it knows not and feels not the influence of revealed truth. They are striking exhibitions of that hardness and tyranny which are congenial to the natural heart, and which break forth in acts of oppression when not restrained by the grace of God. They show how great is man's natural love of despotic power, and that such love cannot be destroyed except by the holy and sanctifying religion of Christ. The absence of the christian religion would fill the world with Neros and Lauds; its prevailing and efficient presence would raise up a host of Melancthons and Howards. The absence of christianity subjects the weaker portion of mankind to the arbitrary will of the stronger; sets tyranny upon the throne of power to exercise remorseless cruelty over the hearts and lives of men. The pervading and active presence of christianity makes all men feel their equality before a just and holy God, and teaches every one's duty to respect the rights of his fellow.

And this is seen to be true, whether we consider the effects of that false system which puts man in the place of God, as is preeminently the case with the church of Rome, and in less degree with every church that has at any time assumed the right to dictate terms of religious belief; or that absolute negation of all religion which prevailed in France, under the reign of heartless infidelity.

Can we doubt, then, from whom our forefathers took lessons in the true principles of freedom? Can we hesitate to declare that those noble men were their instructors, who, in every age and every nation, earnestly and at the expense of everything the world holds dear, contended for those rights and privileges which are the direct inheritance of man from God? Can we doubt that the blessings of human liberty have been preserved to the world by the labors and sufferings of men in the holy cause of christian truth?

Hear what intelligent men have said. The historian, Hume, testifies: "so absolute was the authority of the crown that the precious spark of liberty had been kindled and was preserved by the Puritans alone, and it was to this sect that the English owe the whole freedom of their constitution." The infidel Hume could not appreciate those revealed truths which became living and energizing principles in the hearts of those men he thus praises. With his infidelity he could not understand the nature of the christian faith as an incentive to resist oppression. He knew the fact that the Puritans did contend for the dearest and most exalted rights of man, and he knew that but for them, the British constitution would still be a galling yoke upon the necks of the people. Any man of intelligence might understand that, though he had no appreciation of the faith of the saints which was the secret spring of action to them who would not yield their consciences to the dicta of human tribunals.

Our own historian, Bancroft, hears like testimony. Of Calvin he says, he was "the foremost among the most efficient of modern republican legislators. More truly benevolent to the human race than Solon, more self-denying than Lycurgus, the genius of Calvin infused enduring elements into the constitutions of Geneva, and made it for the modern world, the impregnable fortress of popular liberty, the fertile seed-plot of democracy." Such are the views of men whose religious belief would not incline them to speak with partiality for the defenders of the orthodox faith.

But why thus single out the Puritans and Calvin for praise? They were not the only defenders of human rights. The Scotch Covenanters, the Huguenots of France, the Hussites, the Waldenses and their spiritual progenitors reaching back to the primitive ages of christianity, all of these, and a host of others, as well as our Puritan Fathers, suffered in defending themselves and the world against the aggressive acts of human oppression. Many reformers, as well as Calvin, toiled hard in the cause of popular freedom, that is to say, the freedom of man to believe and act as God requires. The only reason for this distinction is found in the fact that the Puritans were more nearly related to the English people, and had a more immediate influence upon the British constitution, and that Calvin was a more clear and systematic expounder of the common faith of reformed christendom; not that the Puritans or Calvin were truer men, or fought more valiantly than others for the freedom of the human soul.

But there were others who attempted reforms, as well as those to whom reference has been made; and modern times have bestowed no measure of praise upon them. *Voltaire commenced a revolution as well as Luther, and he aimed at the same immediate object, viz: the emancipation of the human mind from the bondage of Rome. Why praise one and execrate the other? Voltaire and Luther both saw the absurdities and corruptions of Rome, and labored to effect a change. Both effected revolutions, but how different in their means and results! Voltaire not only opposed the errors of a despotic church, but also the truths of revelation, and, when his efforts were successful, France became not only free from

*See Dr. Spring's "Power of the Pulpit."

Rome but destitute of all religion. Christianity was nearly dead in the whole nation, her institutions were abolished, and the people were left to the unbridled passions of the depraved heart. There was truly a "reign of terror," for God, the only protector of nations, had been denied an existence; his word, his sabbath, his sanctuary, through which he guards the well-being of a people, were destroyed. After ten years of most wretched experimenting, it was found that infidelity itself could not subsist without christianity in some form and degree, and the nation was forced to return to the embrace of Rome because it had learned no better way.

It is no cause of wonder that the world bestows no praise upon Voltaire and his associates in their infidel attempt at reformation. They secured a liberty, but it was a liberty enshrouded in darkness, gloom and terror; theirs was a freedom, weltering in corruption, and no sun of righteousness rose upon it with healing in his beams.

Luther employed truth to remove error. He saw the world groaning under the oppressive burdens and exactions of a false religion, and he sought to relieve the human mind from its bondage by the agency of a pure christianity. His labors were blessed, and the Reformation spread over Germany, a great part of the continent and the British Isles, carrying virtue and charity and liberty of thought and speech and action in its course; and to day that reformation is sending its blessings to every city, village and town, to every palace, hamlet and cot, from the Atlantic coast to the Pacific shore.

The world has witnessed those two revolutions, so different in all their results to mankind. What were the agents respectively employed, by which one cursed men with a slavery and an intolerance far worse than those of Papal Rome, while the other bequeathed to the world freedom of conscience and security of human rights? These different agents were to be found in the *opinions* of the men who moved and carried forward these changes. The French infidels denied the being of God, and warred against all revealed religion. Luther and his co-laborers loved the sacred truths of scripture, and contended for "the faith once delivered to the saints."

But let us be a little more particular in this statement. The Reformers, amid the fruits of whose labors and sufferings, in behalf of popular freedom, we are now living, were more than Protestants: they were bound together by other and stronger ties than a common opposition to the cruel and absurd tenets of Rome. The christian faith was to them most dear. By it they lived and by it they were armed for conflict with the "Prince of darkness" and the "man of sin."

And what was that faith of the saints for which they so earnestly contended? To present the full investigation of this question, would require far more space than our present limits allow, and we can only briefly mention the results of inquiry. The historian of our country, who has before been quoted, has given the answer, though perhaps unintentionally. This is his statement. "The Pilgrims of Plymouth were Calvinists; the best settlers of South Carolina came from the Calvinists of France; William Penn was the disciple of the Hugeunots; the ships from Holland, that first brought colonies to Manhattan, were filled with Calvinists. He that will not honor the name and respect the influence of Calvin, knows but little of the origin of American liberty."

To be a Calvinist, is to adopt the sentiments of Calvin. And can we say that Calvinism was that form of doctrine which the lion-hearted Reformers and martyrs, in the cause of human freedom, held as that faith which was once delivered to the saints? We can say it, for history fully justifies the assertion. We do not however regard Calvin as the inventor of the doctrines that bear his name. He learned them from the great Apostle to the Gentiles. Paul was a Calvinist, or rather Calvin was a Paulist, and Paul learned the truths by inspiration of the Holy Ghost. At least so we believe; but it is enough for our present purpose to know that the men, to whom we are indebted, under God, for the highest blessings of our freedom, were men who earnestly contended for "the faith once delivered unto the saints," and that the system which we now call Calvanism, embodied their understanding of what the christian faith was. Search the records and you will find that the persecuted for religious opinions' sake, during the dark ages and during the progress of the reformation, held and contended for, those doctrines of grace, which Calvin so fully and systematically explained, while the persecuting powers, whether in Romish or in the English Church, were Armenian in religious sentiment. There were doubtless exceptions to this, but not enough to diminish the force of general truth.

Here is a fact worth knowing, a fact of deep significancy for this church and this nation. Is it true that Calvanism, which is the doctrine of the Presbyterian church, has fought successfully against the tyranny which Paganism and Popery and Infidelity have sought to force upon the human soul? It *is* true. Calvinism *has done* this, it *can* do it, it *will* do it. No nation of true Calvinists can ever be enslaved. That system of faith which exalts God to be the Supreme Sovereign of the Universe, and which brings all men upon the same level of depravity, helplessness and condemnation, and of dependency upon Christ's merits and the work of the Holy Spirit, for salvation, must make men freemen. This system is the great leveller for all mankind, and wars against all oppression by the unwarranted authority of men.

But Calvinism properly embraces something beside purely religious doctrine concerning the fall and salvation of men. The reformer of Geneva also developed, from scripture precept and example, a form of church government, purely representative, purely republican. His system of church polity secured the rights and privileges of the people, by giving them the choice of teachers and rulers. It made the laity all equal and the teachers and rulers all equal, and gave to no men or body of men, an opportunity to exercise irresponsible authority. It was probably to this church polity, that Mr. Barcroft had more especial reference, when he said, "he that will not honor the memory and respect the influence of Calvin, knows but little of the origin of American liberty."

Believe this then, because it is a truth of history which no denial or scepticism can annul. American republicanism has its antecedent in that system of church polity which was chiefly explained and practiced by the great legislator of Geneva. The early settlers of our country, who chiefly gave form to her institutions, were largely taught in the school of Calvin. From him they learned the doctrines of grace; from him they learned the principles of equality and freedom, which are so completely embodied in the constitution of the Presbyterian church, as now established in the United States. The reformed churches of Geneva, Germany, Holland, France and Scotland, were Calvinistic and Presbyterian; and these churches all contributed largely to the settlement of these States. The Puritans, who did so much for the religious and civil well-being of New England, were Calvinists and extensively imbued with the spirit of Presbyterianism.* I scarcely need add that a very important part of the pioneers of this Granite State, were Presbyterians from Ireland.

To Calvinism and Presbyterianism must be traced that love of liberty and independence by which our fathers of the revolution were actuated. Well might the historian, who looks at events in their relation to eternal principles, say that *he* knows but little of the origin of the free institutions of this vast republic, who does not honor and respect the memory of Calvin and his co-laborers and co-sufferers in the cause of religious truth. If you would have confirmation of this, look at the various ecclesiastical organizations of our country, and where you find a church whose creed is most opposed to the doctrines of sovereign grace, as defined in Calvinistic standards, there you will find the most unrepublican church government: and where you find the warmest attachment to, and the most earnest defence of, these same doctrines of grace, there you find the best model of a free government, the firmest adherence to constitutional law, and the least of the spirit of bigotry and sectarianism.

In the midst of your grateful recollections to-day, forget not the goodness of God in bestowing the blessings of civil and religious freedom. Be thankful that he has raised up so many faithful witnesses for christian truth, so many earnest defenders of the faith of the saints, who, whilst strenuously contending for the right to obey God rather than man, bore solemn testimony against human oppression and sealed their testimony with their sufferings and their lives. Be thankful that when the fields of the old world had been drenched in the blood of slaughtered christians, so many of the suffering victims of the demon of intolerance, found a peaceful asylum on these western shores and here laid broad and deep the foundations of constitutional liberty. Be thankful that the founders of this town and church, had been trained in those doctrines and principles, which make tyrants tremble in their seats of power, and inspire the nations with the love of order and liberty. Cherish the church of your fathers—study more and more the sacred truths that have been

* See Neal's History of the Puritans.

here taught—be united in maintaining her polity and her worship—let no dissensions diminish the means of transmitting to posterity the blessings which the faith and polity of this church have secured for the world.

Be thankful that God, in the kindness of his providence, has established the Presbyterian church in this great nation, and, by her greatness, by the completeness of her ecclesiastical organization, by her oneness in the faith and polity of the gospel, has made her one of the most efficient instruments for cementing the bonds between the numerous states of this Union. Be thankful for her ministers, her missionaries, her boards of benevolence, her schools, her colleges, her seminaries, by which she is qualified so extensively to bless this country and the world. Give to her your prayers and your support, that she may, with growing efficiency, bear the sanctifying truths of the gospel and the institutions of civil and religious freedom, to the unfortunate victims of heathenism, superstition and oppression, whether found in our own land, or in the remotest bounds of the earth. Love that faith which was once delivered to the saints, and cherish the memory of those who contended for it even unto death, and thereby transmitted to you and to all the congregations of this commonwealth, the undisturbed privilege of joining the songs of thanksgiving to-day, within this beautious temple of freedom.

I submit this discourse to your serious consideration, with a few reflections. Charity is the fulfilling of the whole law, given for the regulation of human intercourse and the government of human society; but the charity of the gospel rejoices in the truth, and gives life, energy and direction to the belief of the truth. Those who have most earnestly and intelligently contended for the truth, have done it in love. It was burning love that moved Paul to discourse of the faith in Christ so powerfully, that Felix trembled. It was love for the souls of men, a longing for the world's salvation, that prompted the host of christian martyrs, of whom the world was not worthy, earnestly to defend the faith of the saints. Faith when it purifies the heart and overcomes the world, works by love. That love which does not urge to the enforcing of that truth which saves the soul from death, is not christian love. Faith which overlooks the truths of the gospel, which ignores the doctrines of Christ, is not christian faith. Faith which deems religious error harmless, which prefers ease, comfort and peace to a conflict for truth, is a *dead* faith, and is as powerless for the regeneration of the world, as an army of dead soldiers for the storming of a citadel that has a living foe within.

It is not our lot to live in the midst of open persecution for opinion's sake, but it is our lot to witness the evil of a great laxity in doctrine. If charity have not come to hate truth, it at least has numerous and plausible apologies for error. While the professed friends of truth refuse to contend for the faith of the saints as earnestly as the emergency demands, errorists are taking occasions, by their notions, to obstruct the beams which the Sun of righteousness sheds for the enlightening of the world, to poison those fountains whence the stream for the purifying of the nations flows, and to break down those battlements and bulwarks which God has erected for the security of the dearest rights of man.

Let us then receive that faith which God gave to his saints, and, out of love to our fellow men, earnestly contend for it, as occasion requires and strength is given, being assured, both from scripture and from history, that oppression and wrong must hide themselves before the light of the gospel.

www.ingramcontent.com/pod-product-compliance
Lightning Source LLC
LaVergne TN
LVHW020636110826
845149LV00004B/1224

* 9 7 8 1 4 1 8 1 9 1 2 4 5 *